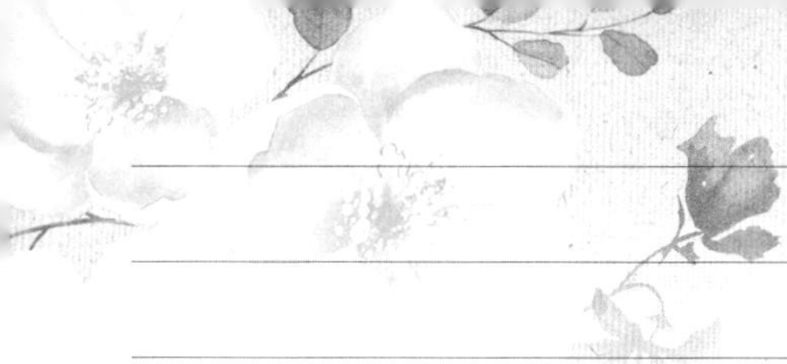

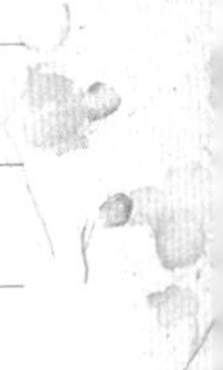

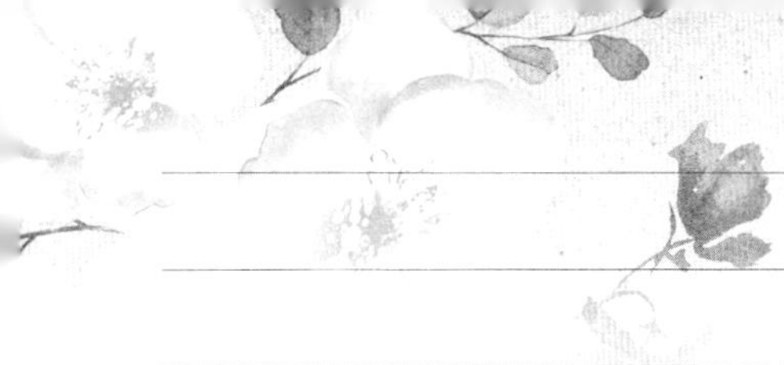

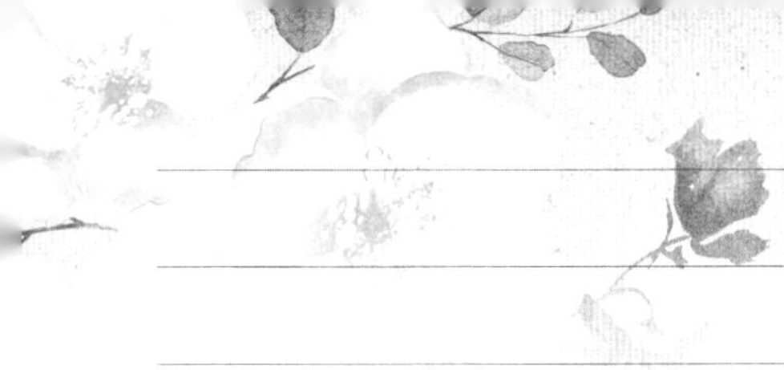

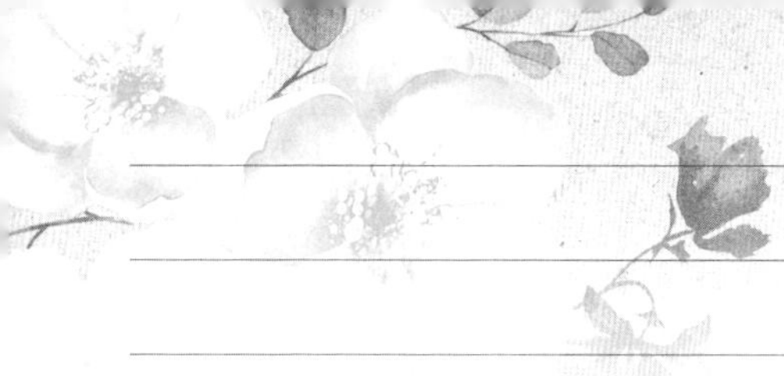

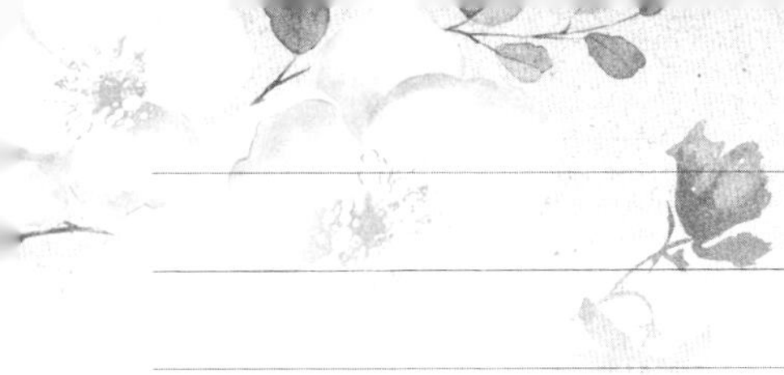

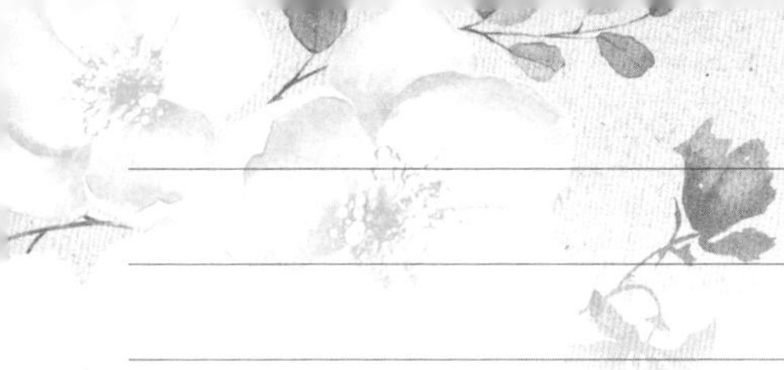

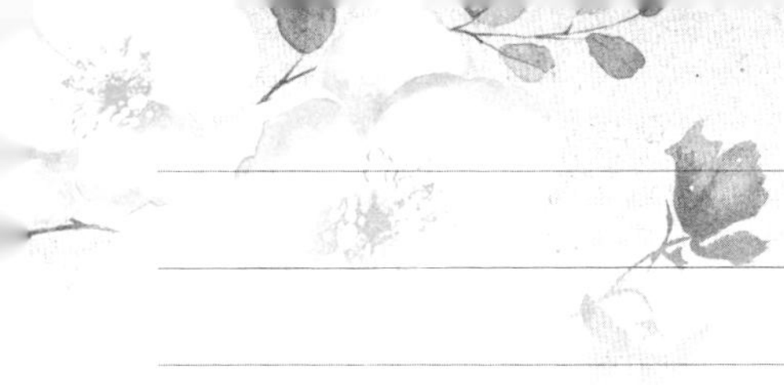

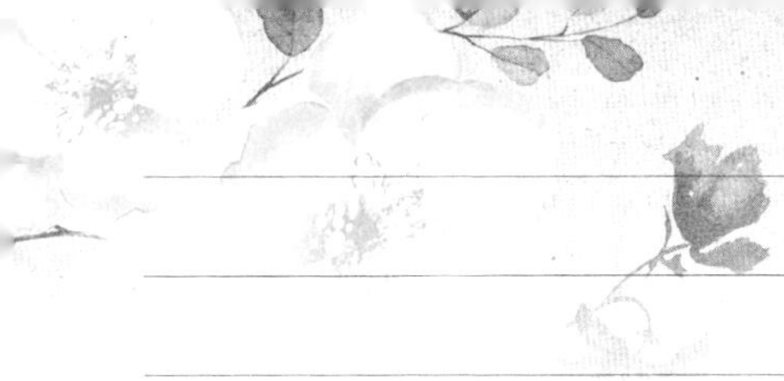

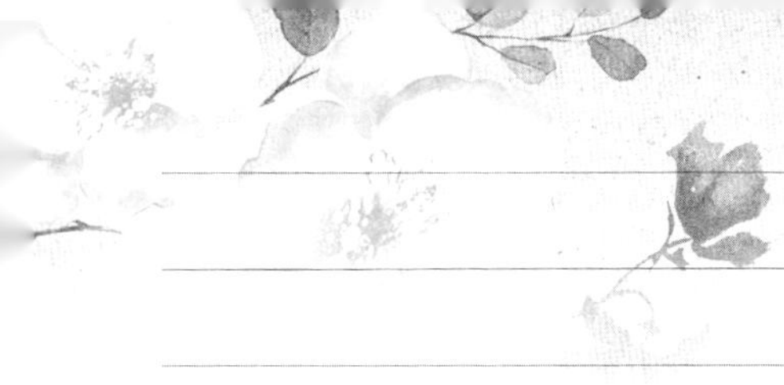

Suppy llists

curtains

plaches